Subterranean Horses

By

YANNIS RITSOS

Illustrations by the Author

Translated by

MINAS SAVVAS

Introduction by

VASSILIS VASSILIKOS

OHIO UNIVERSITY PRESS

Chicago   Athens, Ohio   London

Second Printing, Ohio University Press 1980

ISBN 0-8214-0579-9 clothbound
ISBN 0-8214-0580-2 paperbound
Library of Congress Catalog Card Number 80-83220

FOREWORD

This is the third book in the International
Poetry Forum's Byblos Series. The first was
Marco Antonio Montes de Oca's *The Heart
of the Flute* translated by Laura Villaseñor
with an introduction by Octavio Paz. The
second was Artur Lundkvist's *Agadir* trans-
lated and with an introduction by William
Jay Smith and Leif Sjöberg. This third volume
is in the same tradition of providing the
best translations of some of the most signifi-
cant poets in the world for an audience that
would not otherwise be able to read them
in their own languages.

SAMUEL HAZO
Director

The publication of this book
is made possible by a grant
from Christopher Passodelis
in memory of his parents
Malama and Vasilios Passodelis.

Acknowledgement is also due
for a special grant from The
Hellenic Heritage Foundation.

CONTENTS

INTRODUCTION

The poetry of Yannis Ritsos is as big as the
moon. This collection of translations by
Minas Savvas gives us a small, good sampling
of that moonscape. Even though it may be
difficult for the American reader to appreciate
the full meaning of these lyrics disassociated
from their complete lunar surroundings—a
task that would be less difficult for someone
reading the Greek originals—, these short
samplings of Ritsos' total corpus still speak for
themselves.

One reason for the difficulty is that these
fragments of life transmuted into poetry
by the magical touch of the poet are them-
selves but a part of that totality of the poetic
vision of Ritsos—a vision that achieves its
full perfection in the great narrative poems
and one-act plays. In the original Greek, of
course, they speak forthrightly because the
strength of the language pins them to the
reader's skin. And all translations, even those
as successful as these, do not have the power
of the originals in this sense. Nevertheless,
these poems are characteristic of Ritsos' style.
"A Dog We've Known," for example, can
certainly stand by itself as can many poems
in this collection. Although there are some
others that might appear obscure, such lines as
"His umbrella closed like a sword," "the
baker's light is a sigh that allows a small
passage on the street," "the dull feet of the
dead" and "the uncaressed dog sniffs the
clothes of the dead woman" remain un-
mistakably Ritsos.

Yannis Ritsos is today an active and

[*xi*]

productive poet. Like the sun he is in rapport
with the moon of his poetry. In Greece his
enlightened personality and his moral and
ethical courage are examples that are not
often seen. Now that his reputation has
gone beyond his homeland, some are saying
that there is a lot of Ritsos translated today.
Almost too much. Perhaps this is true. But
what about the thirty-year silence that walled
in his poetry for Greek audiences only or
for the audiences of socialist countries? One
wonders if a poet must bleed first before
he earns the right to be translated or before
so-called hellenists rise from their monu-
mental indifference and recognize him?
Such is the case of Yannis Ritsos. It took his
second crucifixion (the first having occurred
during the Greek Civil War) to arouse the
delayed interest of western translators and
publishers. So I say that it is not that too
much of the poetry of Ritsos has been trans-
lated, but it is still not enough. Additional
translations of his work would be more than
welcome.

All students of modern Greece know
that Monovassia, which is Ritsos' birthplace,
was a symbol of freedom and revolt during
the Greek War of Independence. The art of
Yannis Ritsos is the Monovassia of modern
Greek poetry.

VASSILIS VASSILIKOS

Subterranean Horses

EQUIVALENCE

Then at once the wind stopped.
Someone turned off the bath's faucet.
The mystical symphony had ended.
The man, with his finger upon his lips,
motioned yes. The small-bodied woman
made the sign of the cross
upon the child, asleep
between a lithograph of Apollo
and a satin stitch of the crucified Christ.

EMPTY BOTTLES

These empty beer bottles and those others
of wine, of lemonade or oil, down in the
      basement,
lie amidst wooden boxes, dusty, molded—.

If you could take them out one day under
      sunshine—
no need to wash them—if only they were
      warmed a little
if only the shadow of a bird could brush
      their sides—

No! It's not another excuse. I'm speaking
about those bottles, years in the basement.
      One of them
had, I think, two strange glass hands
and was pressing on her temples as if she
      had a headache.

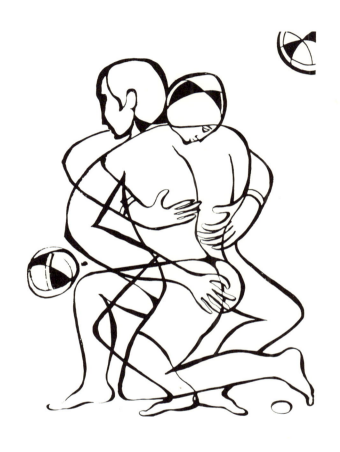

SO?

"You would have been more sincere, of
    course, if you had died,
if you had . . ." she did not continue. She
    watched him undress
as usual, pulling off his clothing piece by
    piece. When he was
completely naked, he crossed the room,
    wound the alarm clock,
walked into the kitchen and returned with a
    glass of water.
Still naked, he placed the glass on the dresser.
He smiled. "So?" he said only.
"So?" And he dipped one finger in the glass.

THE POEM

The garbage dump under the Planetarium—
and the madman alone beats
a rusty old can in fine accompaniment
with the stars and with the keys
of the old switchman who keeps awake
next to the rails of the unserviceable train
where the nasty nettles grow,
hiding the boots of the soldier who undressed
so as to climb and stand erect
upon the pediment of the ancient temple.

REVERENT COMPARISON

Next to each other, the pharmacy, the pastry
    shop, the coffeehouse,
farther down the small flower shop. The
    people do not stop.
The women stare at the glass of the store-
    windows before the arrival of darkness.

Behind the half-built wall, in the abandoned
    soccer-field with the hollyhocks,
everyone discards his own kind of trash—
    cardboard discs,
vials from drugs, broken cups, water glasses,
rotten flowers.
                There gather the old women
    and the dogs.
They rummage in the piles carefully, absent-
    mindedly; they do not notice
the golden twilight; they search like the
    poets for the poem,
these most bitter old women, these forsaken
    women, so happy
with a dried orange peeling, a piece of
    broken mirror,
with a blue tube from the pharmacy, a tube
    upon which still visible
are the traces of the homeless snail, a tube
in whose cavity can be heard the sounds of
    the train heading for Larisa.

MEETING

Nothing, of course, comes totally by itself.
You also must search to find it. In the
      mornings
the sun enters from the eastern window, it
      bleaches
the two purple arm-chairs, pauses a little
      and withdraws,
leaving behind a suggestion of gentleness
      —that calm erasing.
      And the flowers of the carpet,
condemned to footsteps, have their rights;
with ears glued to the carpet, they listen
to the rhythmic galloping of the subterranean
      horses. Then
the reticent woman enters, and you can see
that she is careful not to step on those flowers.

The ungraspable can perhaps be endured by
      two together,
but it is never revealed except to one alone.

A DOG WE'VE KNOWN

We've known that dog for years—
   always the same,
always with a large bone in his mouth—
   neither chewing it
nor releasing it from his jaws (and how
   could he bark now?)—
unless at night, while we're asleep, he,
   in hiding,
grinds on it secretly, and then digging
   somewhere (who knows?)
he finds a new bone for the next day;
   or perhaps
he has learned that barking is of no use,
that it protects nothing, neither the house
   nor the yard
or the fountain or himself, from the moon,
   from time,
from thieves.

THE SECRET SENTRY

They waited in the town square. In the center
they had erected a platform. Paper lanterns,
paper flags hung over the columns.
In the afternoon came a heavy rain. The
      square
was filled with black umbrellas and soaking
      shoes.
No faces could be seen. It turned dark.
The one who was to speak did not arrive.
      Then,
one by one, slowly, in order, they moved,
closed their umbrellas, placing them on
      the platform,
and walked away in the rain under the
      lamp-posts.
Only the last one, with the huge mask,
remained guarding the platform, holding
his umbrella closed like a sword
amidst the wet paper flags.

COUNTERFEITING

The empty drawers yawned after the search.
Imprints of deep breathing on the mirror
    of the dark room . . .
Across the street the bright shop-window of
    the butcher-shop
and the old hand-barrow with the old
    wax-replica
of Alexander the Great, without spear or
    helmet,
lying supine amidst the rotten oranges . . .

OF THE AFTERNOON

The chickens were still pecking in the street.
    The guerrilla's mother
sat on the door-step holding her grandson
    on her parted knees.
A boy was carrying a straw basket. The huts
    were spread out confusedly
containing old trunks, iron beds, tables,
    wooden frames. A phonograph
played hoarsely within a bolted room. The
    bed-sheets
in wide squares contained their history. The
    sea could not be heard.
A large, invisible hand lifted the chairs several
    inches above the ground.
How can humans live without poetry?

BECAUSE

Because the buses were idle before the fence,
because the mannequins gesticulated in the
    lighted shop-windows,
because the girl with the bicycle
    procrastinated before the pharmacy,
because the woodsman smashed the glass-door
    of the beer-tavern,
because the boy with the stolen pencil was
    alone in the elevator,
because the dogs had been abandoned next
    to the seaside villas,
because the rusty grater was covered by the
    nettles,
because the sky was ashen with a scarlet fish,
because the horse on the mountain was more
    alone than the star,
because both they and these others were
    hunted—
for this, only for this reason I lied to you.

PREPARATION FOR A CEREMONY

Something is not right with the event
    they've prepared for me.
They go up and down stairways; they
    gather on corridors.
The three chandeliers of the large banquet
    room are lit.
On the rostrum the glass with the water
    glitters. They introduce me.
I force my legs; my hands search for me. I am
    missing.
And even if I were to descend those steps,
    the policeman would arrest me.

THE TWO VIEWS

A handful of bones and a piece of rusty
iron . . . the woman
gathered greens at the farm. Her legs could
    be seen
up to the thighs. Farther down
the dog guarded the baby under the tree.
When dusk arrived,
we returned to town, stood before the red
    house
and stared through the lower window.
    The two were
seated at the table next to the lamp;
the dinner dishes, slow movements—a silent
rancour. The third one standing
over them peeled an apple with a knife.
And just then
he turned and said: "We always end on the
    same thing,"
and perhaps by that he meant
Original Sin or that he had forgotten his comb
in an unfamiliar bathroom.

DESCENT

"Eurydice!" he shouted. He descended the
    stairway hastily.
The caretaker's quarters were without light.
    He probed the mirror with his hands.
In the depths, the woman with the yellow
    umbrella was departing.
The second woman shouted back to him
    from the basement: "She is dead."
The three airmen came out of the elevator
    with a suitcase—
in it were her two severed hands and my
    manuscript.

INSIGNIFICANT NEEDS

The houses jam one on top of the other,
or face to face, without exchanging glances.
    The elbows
of the chimneys shove each other in the night.
    The baker's light
is a sigh that allows a small passage on the
    street.
A cat looks behind her. Vanishes. A man
enters his room. On his blanket,
over his iron bed, he finds reclining
the crowded desolation of the city. As he
    undresses,
he recalls that he hasn't noticed if there is
    a moon.
The bulks of the houses are shuffling in
    his memory
like cards in a closed, secretive gambling room
where all the players have lost. And he
    needs to imagine
that someone must love him, within these
    numberless houses, ·
so that he can sleep, so that he can wake up.
But, yes, of course, there is a moon,—
    he remembers
the illumination of a ditch with soap-water.

NECESSARY EXPLANATION

There are some stanzas—sometimes
     whole poems—
that neither I can explain. What I do not know
still sustains me. And you're justified in
     asking. Don't ask me.
I don't know, I tell you.
                  Two parallel lights
from the same night-club. The sound of water
in winter, falling from the overflowing
     cistern,
or the sound of a water-drop as it falls
from a rose upon the sprinkled garden
slowly, slowly during a spring evening
like the sob of a bird. I don't know
what that sound means; yet I accept it.
Whatever else I know I explain to you.
     I do not neglect it.
But these also add to our life. I was gazing,
as she slept, at her knee making a corner
     on the sheet—
It wasn't only love. That corner
was the veiled line of tenderness, and the
     aroma
of the sheet, of neatness and of spring,
     completed
that inexplicable thing which I sought,
     in vain again,
to explain to you.

CALCULATED BEHAVIOR

He was measuring his gestures, his grimaces,
    his words,
even at night when, alone, in his narrow room
he was arranging his shoes, his clothes,
    moving
from his bed to the closet. And if at midnight,
    occasionally,
he would undress completely and stare
    erotically at his nudity
before the mirror, he would do so in
    order to pretend
that he did not know that the big voyeur
    and eavesdropper
from the empty, unrented room next door,
with the nails on the wall, would always
    watch him
through the invisible holes on the door or
    those on his own body.

IN THE OLD GARDEN

She stood up, after many years, the sick
    woman,
and went out in the garden. Winter sunshine.
    Encircled serenity—
upon it glide the blows on nails driven into
    invisible
new scaffolds. There is odor in the grass.
    Flower-pots, stone-walls
frayed by shaggy plants and roots. The
    pomegranate-tree
taller than the cypress. The well is shut.
    Yellow dust
like that falling behind punctured icons.
    And suddenly
the distant nuptial fragrance of cool orange-
    blossoms
handsomely arranged in a tray of silver
upon the pedestal of a proud statue that is
    absent.

BY DEFAULT

Dusty glass windows with fraudulent
    reflections
from a conventional sunburst. A painted
    woman
shakes a red sheet from the window,
then she moves back inside, as if she finished
a performance which we did not see. Below
on the sidewalk, the cigarette butts remain
with bitten, twisted, red filter-tips.

THE FUNDAMENTALS

Clumsily, with thick needle, thick thread,
he sews the buttons on his coat; he speaks
    to himself:

"Did you eat your bread? Sleep well?
Were you able to speak? To extend your arm?
Did you remember to look out of the
    window?
Did you smile at the knock on the door?
If it's always death, he is a late-comer.
Freedom always comes first."

HARVEST OF SPACE

Tall plane-trees, muscular torsos of coolness.
The shade is not intended to hide anything.
Brave light, brave shade—
useless daring—to counter what?—
simplicity breathes in the air.

People sit under the trees,
they dine on small wooden tables, they talk,
they do not suspect the magnitude covering
    them, the magnitude
that regulates their innocent gestures.
    Toward evening
someone (maybe drunk) sings. The plane-trees
move in a silent procession toward the
    horizon.
The area empties. The waiter, with his
    white apron,
appears for a moment at a distance, in the
    crimson dusk,
holding in priestly fashion the tray with
    the empty glasses.

PIRAEUS DETAINEES' TRANSPORT STATION

Half of the blanket is under, half over—
	fever, cement, dampness,
soggy hair, writing on the walls inscribed
	with fingernails—
names, dates, small promises; the same torch
	makes holes
in the same nightmare: "Tonight."
	"Tonight."
"Tomorrow at dawn." Who will remain
	here to remember us
when the key will be heard in the lock and
	the long chain
will be dragged on the endless whiteness
	where, in a corner,
the last cigarette we discarded still smokes?

DISTURBANCE

Soldiers with large dirty feet mingle
with their blankets, with their breath,
    with the rancid air,
just as a secretive moon rises and as bullets
    burst
below by the slaughter-house—"Thanasi!
    Thanasi!"*
shout the women behind the shutters. No one
turns to look—lost names, lost consciences;
dogs roll the clay-jugs on the road; drums
    of steel
tumble from the hills. "Thanasi! Thanasi!"
And a cluster of leaflets burst from the
    blindman's hat
as he tries to protect his violin under his coat.

*Thanasi is the modern diminutive of Athanassios. Ritsos
is exploiting the fact that Thanasi (the normal addressive
form of this male name) connotes death while Athanassios
derives from the word for immortality. (Translator's note.)

SECRET RITUAL

Her footsteps echoed. They announced
    her presence.
Like her hands.
She had thought of saying something else,
    but couldn't.
But it was even worse just saying that.

So that finally, unseen, naked,
she stood before the yawning doorway
and with terse, interrupted movements,
    like any housewife,
she brushed an old coat she would never wear.

A SICK MAN'S REWARD

A smell of humid, rotten planks all through
     the day,
drying and smoking on the blatant sun.
     Some birds
gaze from a roof and in an instant fly away.
In a neighborhood taverna, in the evening,
     the grave-diggers gather.
They eat fried foods. They drink. They sing
a song full of grim gaps,
and through those gaps, a quiet wind begins
     to blow;
and the leaves, the lamps, the papers on the
     shelves begin to tremble.

WOMEN

Women often seem distant. Their sheets
    smell of "Goodnight."
They place the bread on the table so that
    we can ignore their absence.
Then we realize our guilt. We rise from the
    chair and say:
"You must have gotten very tired today," or
    "That's all right, I'll light the lamp."
When we strike the match, she turns,
    slowly moving
with inexplicable devotion toward the
    kitchen. Her back
is a tiny but bitter hill, carrying the dead,
the dead of the family, her own dead and
    yours.
You listen to her footsteps creaking on the
    aged planks of the floor.
You listen to the dishes weeping on the
    shelves, and then you hear
the howl of the train, transporting the soldiers
    to the front.

A MAN

A strange man, truly, with a preposterous
    glance,
with a preposterous gait. Within his body
    (we knew it for sure)
he had gathered, not any images, no
    duplicates, but the things themselves—
those comely, pine-covered mountains the
    hill with the three pillars,
the olive grove below the hill, the red horse,
    the steps
carved upon the rock leading to the house
    that emits smoke,
the two wine glasses on the silver tray.
    Whenever they lock him up, he climbs
those pine-covered mountains (within his
    body), he sits on the rock,
he stares at the seas and strokes a platan-leaf
    upon his knee
as if he is flattening a letter rumpled in anger
    and in sadness.

SUSPENSION

She touched the empty dress, hung on the
    wall for years.
Little by little the dress swelled—already
    visible
were the two small circles on the knees,
    the breasts, the hips,
when the servant's sneeze was heard in the
    inner doorway.
She thought he was asleep. The mirror
darkened from an unknown breath. The
    dress had fallen
totally empty on the floor, next to the
    paper flowers.

COINCIDENCES

The chairs had an expression as if they
    waited for someone in the night.
The clock suddenly stopped, and from the
    next room by itself
sounded the old guitar, hanging on the wall;
    that sound
melted slowly within the house like a piece
    of chocolate
under the pillow of an ailing child. Exactly
    then
the old man stood up shouting: "Speak out,
    at last. Speak!"
The woman said nothing. She entered the
    other room, covered the guitar
with an old sheet, while the raindrops were
    already striking the roof.

SELF-SYMPATHY

He sits on the chair. He wants to be tranquil.
    He is.
This is a door. This, a window. He
    distinguishes them. Fine.
There are houses, streets, a garden; over
    the fence
a red leaf trembles for a moment. At night
nothing is seen. Yet, they are there. He rises.
    Lights the lamp.
Washes the cup, pours new water into the
    coffee pot.
Sacred, persevering movements of mankind.
    The tiny lizard
there, on the wall, next to the roof, watches,
    agrees.

REFUTATION

So all is not lost. The window
still reveals a piece of the city, a piece
of almost available sky. The carpenter,
        the bricklayer,
suspended upon the scaffold, come again
        nearer.
Nails and boards then have another function,
and dreams again and the minutest
        resurrection
and sorrowful glory, useful once again,
        recalling
those toothpicks in the vest pocket
which so many years ago we had taken
        secretly
from that humble restaurant one winter night.

REVIEW

The one who slept with his shoes and his
    clothes on,
soaked to the bone, and the other one
who stuck his head in the black sack,
sensing the hardness of the cloth on his chin,
    the one
who had stolen the shoes of the corpse in
    the bedroom—
they were too tight, he did not wear them
and couldn't sell them, lest he be betrayed—
and that last one who tapped his foot
    incessantly
on the rotten planks in a rhythm we could
    all recognize
but which no one would name. . . . Then,
    above,
the smoking wick-lamp and the shouts
    of drunks
and gamblers, the large bronze ashtray with
    a carving
of the Prince of Lilies,—and then
the stern, hermetic, bony waiter
with a movement of his left hand sweeping
the whole table, dropping into the doortrap
glasses, cards, cigarette packs; and the
    customers,
astonished, exchanging hurried anger
in hypnotized communion, their foreheads
    glistening
from the crystal chandelier which brightened
    suddenly
there at the deep interior, behind an unknown
    glass door
in the empty, enormous room of the
    dignitaries . . .

A GESTURE

Here is something again that unexpectedly
    you like, something
insignificant like the gesture of the woman
who pulls out of the vase the withered
    flowers—
she does not throw them away; she pauses,
    wonders;
a hesitant gesture regretted before the fact—
if you speak to her, she will not hear—
    a gesture
entirely muted, like the word you put in
    the poem
and then you turn and ask, "Did you say
    something?"
And you do not care that war was declared
and that the large airplanes carve the twilight
with dark, two-edged shadows amidst
    the redness.

AND ONE MORE NIGHT

That silver candlestick was placed
between two spaces. He tried
to blow out the candle and lie down. Then
he noticed the tension of his breath
upon the resistance of the flame—he noted
the curve of this flame—a slight bow
(for him?), a kind of acquiescence
and then the trembling rise upward.
  He did not lie down.
He stood there watching in that flame's
   interior,
in an immeasurable, forgotten depth,
that same body, naked, invulnerable
in fresh resurgence, not at all illuminated,
while on the right foot of the ascending body
that same rope was tied, still trailing.

IMPROVISED CONFIGURATION

Perhaps the houses do grow. Men, contrarily,
diminish by the day. In the elevator
the three naked women, laughing, carry
    upstairs
a huge portrait of an old bearded man
while, reflected in the mirror, glitter
the wide thighs and the breasts of one of them
and the lusterless spine of the frame with
    the tiny spiders
and the triangular, moth-eaten string
    dragging behind.

DIFFICULT ADMISSION

I bought the logs and the nails. Do not
    betray me.
I didn't even have to tell you. But I must.
    When the others,
naked under the sun, were hammering in the
    nails, He ascended
fully dressed, even with his necktie. He
    unfolded the script,
the great outline, pointing to the scroll.
He made me freeze. The hammers stopped
    altogether.

Now I know at last the difference between
    iron and paper. The world
is divided in two. Say what you will, it will
    never unite.

AFTER AN INTERRUPTION

When, after years, he sat down to write
    something,
he suddently felt neglected, unwashed,
    forsaken,
like the unmarried woman who, occupied
    all day
with the chores of the house, passes by the
    mirror
at night and as her glance falls upon
her unkempt image she suddenly recalls
that all day she did not at all look in the
    mirror:

has she aged so much then? Has she died
    already? Why
should she comb her hair now?—the day is
    over. No one
will see her—no one now. Yet she raises
    the black comb
and begins to comb her long hair downward,
as if she is combing a girlfriend's corpse, a
    girlfriend beloved
and suddenly so alien, with her eyes closed—
and that wart on the nose.

ERRORS

The man was sitting on the sofa, speaking;
he would listen to his voice, correcting the
    tone.
The woman was arranging her hair before
    the mirror.

The woman's hair was dyed.
The man's voice was dyed. They knew it.

They turned off the lights and fell to their
    knees.
Later they made love on the floor. And
    outside,
the old woman was knocking on the iron gate.

IN THE BASEMENT HALLWAY

These springs of old couches, these twisted
    wires
dressed in the austerity of rust, abandoned
in the hallway underground—years in
    uselessness.
Sunday noon you would say: "My best, sir,
    how's the wife?"
for you had to say something, though no one
    else could hear.
You'd look out of the basement window at
    the dull feet of the dead
with their shoes freshly polished; and on the
    floor below,
still smelling of the old, spilled must, there
    was a severed hand
tied to a yellow string, and another hand from
    a cavity in the wall
pulled at the string, causing the other hand
    to jump
clumsily, unexpectedly, sadly, somewhat
    comically—it was a jump
higher than it was natural—a jump as if not
    of this world.

ISOLATION

He crawled into the hole of his own shadow,
    like a wounded dog
inhaling his own breath in all its soothing
    warmth,
alone, accompanied by his being, his aliveness,
loyal and bold, as if for ever determined.

So, crouched into a perfect circle
he was a well's mouth, pointing downward
at the dark, deep silence, knowing with a
    feeling of relief
that he was out of the well.

AIMLESS PERSISTENCE

He mixes the clay; his hands tremble;
    he is scared;
he can think of nothing to create. The house
    is empty. Perhaps he should
depict the face of fear, or the hands of fear
with his own hands as models—but they
    are hidden,
buried in the mud. Only an enormous eye,
a red eye fixed on him, does not allow him
to see anything else. He takes the knife.
    Stabs the clay. Waits.
The clay is drying with the knife stuck on
    its side.
It dries on his fingers too—he can't move
    them.

Is this his statue then? The large, uncaressed
    dog
sniffs the clothes of the dead woman, crawls
    under the table and whimpers.

CELEBRATION

They closed the schools. Before the doors
    they placed large wreaths.
In the dressing room of the soccer field there
    was a pile of soldiers' uniforms.
They brought the statue secretly at night
    to the higher public square;
they placed a soldier's cap on it—they
    promoted it, it was said. "Ah, think
that statue, the (only) nude one, with a
    golden cap." he said.
Besides, who would look at it, in such tumult,
    in the noon of day?
The people did not raise their heads, so that no
    one might think that they were looking.
He stared at his nails. How they had grown,
    really.

RESISTANCE

He still resists; he tries to count accurately;
    he arranges
the odd numbers in one place, the even in
    another. Upon retiring,
when huge shadows burglarize his sleep,
    he places them
under his pillow. The next day, he pulls
    them out,
spreads them on the table, lights a cigarette
    and begins to write.
Under this table he is well aware stand his
    feet with iron shoes,
and under his shoes the earth stretches to
    her farthest end.

OBSERVATION POINT

That serenity, that speechlessness of the most
    prolonged compassion,
along with the key of the demolished house,
    and the interior ladder,
and the stool, and the golden ashtray—
    you have no one to whom to give them.
You sit by the window, behind the grilles.
    You gaze at the street.
The horse carriage passes by the old knife
    grinder, the street cleaner, the customs
    officer.
The girl has black hair. The crippled man
    hobbles even more
as he tries not to hobble. You want to tell
    him about it. He
pauses for a minute, raises his head. He must
    have certainly
seen your face carved with golden lines from
    the grilles,
and perhaps that is why he smiled. He walks
    again. He does not pretend.
He hobbles so freely now that he no longer
    hobbles. And you
imagine your face within his eyes as pale,
    sanctified
with two tight cracks between your eyes.
    In the meantime, you hesitate
to rise and stare in the mirror, lest the
    golden lines
vanish from your face and you're left with
    the black lines
upon which the spider clutches as it descends
    even deeper.

CHANGE OF RESIDENCE

Mothers were dying early. How did we grow
in strange arms? Winter mornings with a
    chunk
of bread sprinkled with moist sugar. The
    alarm clocks
would sever our sleep in half. We would go on
    the street unwashed.
We changed homes often, always leaving
    something behind—
a locker with some books, a broken
    mandoline . . .
"Some Sunday," we would say, "we'll drop
    by to pick them up."
We never did. And in that thin suitcase,
in the center of the room, torn and faded,
with the straps spread out on the floor,
we had forgotten an old protective-amulet
    with black string
along with those excessively-seen obscene
    photographs
of naked women from a bygone era—
    women of wide pelvises,
slim waists and enormous breasts.
                           One of them
had fallen prostrate as if weeping. And, truly,
    she cried
before the wall with the rusty nails
upon which hung the opened scissors and
    the suspenders.

STORY

All the plans were of no use—every so often
    they were overturned,
like that bus on its way to an outing,—
    most of them were killed,
the rest were carried to the nearest hospital;
    a wheel
rolled down hill; a boy found it; he made a
    crude hand-barrow;
now he roams the suburbs with it, selling
    oranges; the oranges glitter,
a mound of insignificant suns. So simply
    we pass. So simply
we speak, we forget, get accustomed.
    So simply they forget us.

COLLATERALS

The money-exchanger's counter of glass—
    what
strange coins, what dentures of gold
of silver, or iron, and individual crowns of
    the dead, Helen's necklace,
a large hatpin, the Old Testament
    with silver binding,
with red and green stones. The large clock of
    City Hall struck twelve.
They were taking the fowl out of the freezer.
The shoe-shine boy stood at the doorway
with Antinöos' boots through his hands. Then
a small wind sighed from the south; it
    fluttered the sheet. Under the bed
the white slipper of the dead bride came
    into view.

SPRING 1971

The man had gone to work some time ago.
    The woman
entered the bedroom, opened the drawer
    and took out
the bills for the water, the electricity, the
    telephone,
turning her back to the balcony door. "Let
    them discontinue
everything, everything," she cried, "let them
    stop everything"—as if she
didn't know that they had already stopped
    everything.
                A swollen sun
flooded the large bed. The shadow was
    evaporating
upon the opposite wall. A fly sat upon the
    cake in the ashtray,
on the alarm-clock, on the blue ribbon
of the dead child. The two light-filled sheets
seemed like two blinded statues, lying down
for unappetizing morning sex.
    "Everything, everything," she said again
and within "everything" (she heard it) she,
    too, was included,
silent, peaceful, erect, liberated, united
with all that was ruined, whether extinguished
    or existing.

IN THE OLD NEIGHBORHOOD

They take the tables of the cafe out on the
    sidewalk.
The old men in the afternoon come and sit
    down. The sunshine
reclines upon the newspapers, wipes away
    the news.
They can no longer read; perhaps they would
    even get mad,
perhaps they forget easily—for Death always
    occupies
the back of the newspapers as he occupies
those backyards with the wells shut.
And the afternoon is quiet in the old
    neighborhood
as if, long ago, all the pregnant women had
    moved out.

SUCH WHITENESS

Behind the glass partition, the shop glitters
      whiteness—
white walls, white benches, and on the
      benches
white cases with white eggs. Only
a large black fly was knocking on the glass.
And you, you were convinced that the
      shopkeeper
had died awhile ago in the bathroom
with the coins from the last of the sales
in his pockets—such unused whiteness,
such unsought whiteness, lonely, blinding.

BEAUTY

Naked, she took the red handkerchief
and covered her eyes so as not to be seen
in case fear would force them to look.
Silent and arrogant—maybe even afraid,
within the darkness of her concealed eyes,
she may have even touched or even mixed
     the light.
Then she did not wake.

Under the straw-chair of the garden, her
     shoes remained
with the bare form of her feet. On the tree-
     branch,
her white dress streamed, unfastening all
     her nudity.

She had hoped for this after death. The light
     of the garden
fluttered—I don't know how—like mocking,
     like applause.

THE SURVIVORS

The dead forget, are forgotten.
In the closets their clothes dissolve.
The dead woman was carried to the morgue.
The canaries above the stairs were shrieking.
The neighbor-women were gesturing
        through the windows.
The garbage-man came by on time.
The bell, the trash cans, the paper plates,
the rotten lettuce leaves, the red string.
The hands filthy in the pockets.
The newlyweds entered the photography
        studio.
Then suddenly it was noon. Everything was
        snuffed out. The blind man,
unshaven, stooping, was still watching
through the keyhole of the nailed door.

IN THE VOID

This dripping of water on the rock
and the sound of water
in the winter's sun—
a voice
of a lonely bird
within the hollow sky
searching for us once again,
understanding again
(understanding which "yes"?)
as it falls from the heights
upon the buses parked
with the dead, tourists for centuries.

CHURCH-BELLS

Do you remember the church-bells charging
    through the rooms, on Sunday, a holiday,
stirring the children's hair and the sheets?
    Then
cold water was good for faces, and the smell
    of coffee in the kitchen—
the whole house steamed from the
    evaporation of the night in the sun,
and the flies sat on the window glass and
    stared out toward the yard in confusion,
not knowing who tapped them amicably
    on one shoulder. Now
these church-bells, hanging in the line amidst
    the dampness,
are like the black hats of the dead, the remote
    dead—they don't peal;
the storks pass by, drop their excrement on
    them, and fly south.

THE CEMETERY STATUES

The statues naked under the trees of the
      cemeteries
are conquered by the frantic voices of the
      night-birds
when the last of the procession disappear.
      The statues
convincingly imitate death, love, the
      tranquility,
with an iron lantern in hand, with a
      marble lily,
with swords of stone, with stone wings,
      stone flags,
from the hither to here, to elsewhere; lighted
      windows,
beds, a nocturnal dance in the yard.
      "Go away, go away!"
Peter shrieked, "the caretaker has my keys
      in his belt;
his dog chases me—it is my rejection.
      The statues
do not imitate us; they are also lonely; they're
      in pain;
they deny non-being, they're enflamed,
      reddened;
their central vein swells with blood.
This is why even the birds cry so much—so as
to disguise the defeat of pacifying death."

AFTER EVERY DEATH

Searching again, and again from the
    beginning, for that immensely smooth
for that excessively round object—the white
    pebble so long forgotten; kept
in the black Navy coffer—the woman was
    bent over the window
pressing her left breast upon the wood. In the
    conduit
of the roof across the way the red bullet
    had stopped.
"I was thinking," she sighed, listening sadly
    to her own voice,
staring at the statue on the garden below,
    "of the one
they brought up from the sea with the help
    of many
acetylene lamps. How he ascended
with his fresh thickened thumb upon his
moist lips,
blocking their exquisite abbreviated whiteness
before they could express themselves."

THE DISTANT

O distant, distant; depth unapproachable;
    you always greet
the silent ones in their absence, in the absence
    of others,
when danger from the immediate
    immediately burdens
in promising nights with multicolored lights
    in gardens,
when the eyes of lions and tigers phosphorize
    half-closed
with green intermittent silences behind
    their cages
and when the old clown before the darkened
    mirror
wipes away his painted tears in order to cry.
O, peace ungiveable, you with the long,
    moist hand,
invisible peace, without borrowing, without
    debts,
hammering nails on the sin, stabilizing the
    world
within that nether indolence where music
    reigns.

Vitae

YANNIS RITSOS was born May 19, 1909 in
Monovassia. As a result of a life full of personal
and national tragedy, Ritsos devoted his life
to poetry and revolutionary socialism. He has
authored 52 volumes of poems and has been
translated into 25 languages. English translations
in collections include *Selected Poems, Gestures and
Other Poems, Selected Poetry of Ritsos, Chronicle
of Exile, In Parentheses, The Lady of the Vineyards*
and *Scripture of the Blind*. Ritsos was awarded the
Lenin Peace Prize in 1977, and has been nominated
for the Nobel Prize in literature three times.

MINAS SAVVAS, a critic, poet and translator, is
also a Professor of Literature at San Diego State
University. He has published one book of
verse, dozens of reviews and articles, and trans-
lations from modern Greek literature. His
translations of the poetry of Yannis Ritsos have
appeared in *The New York Review of Books,
Chicago Review, Texas Quarterly, The Minnesota
Review, Translation, Praxis, Antioch Review,
Boundary 2, Antaeus,* etc. In 1977 he published a
volume of Ritsos' poetry in translation under
the title of *Chronicle of Exile*.

VASSILIS VASSILIKOS, who was born in Kavala,
Greece, in 1933, has published in Greek some
twenty prose works as well as a half-dozen
selections of poetry. Earlier books of his to appear
in the United States include *The Plant, The Well,
The Angel*, which has been translated into
sixteen languages; *The Photographs,* translated
into ten; and *Z,* translated into thirty-two and
made into a motion picture of the same title.

The Harpoon Gun, Outside the Walls and *The Monarch* are his most recent books.

As the recipient of a Ford Foundation grant, Vassilikos traveled throughout the United States in 1959. From 1967 until 1974 he was an exile from his native land, dividing his time between Paris and Rome. He presently lives in Athens.

Originally published as Volume III of the Byblos Editions, International Poetry Forum, in a limited edition of two hundred and thirty copies. The text is set in Monotype Bembo, and the display type on the title page is Chisel by Stephenson Blacke, composed by Davis & Warde, Inc., Pittsburgh, Pa. Designed by Thomas C. Pears III.